THE EXCHANGE

JAN 1 8 2014

The Exch

Poetry by

SOPHIE CABOT BLACK

Graywolf Press

JACKSON COUNTY LIBRARY SERVICES

MEDFORD, OREGON 97501

Copyright © 2013 by Sophie Cabot Black

This publication is made possible, in part, by the voters of Minnesota through a Minnesota State Arts Board Operating Support grant, thanks to a legislative appropriation from the arts and cultural heritage fund, and through a grant from the National Endowment for the Arts. Significant support has also been provided by Target, the McKnight Foundation, Amazon.com, and other generous contributions from foundations, corporations, and individuals. To these organizations and individuals we offer our heartfelt thanks.

Published by Graywolf Press
250 Third Avenue North, Suite 600
Minneapolis, Minnesota 55401

All rights reserved.

www.graywolfpress.org

Published in the United States of America

ISBN 978-1-55597-641-5

2   4   6   8   9   7   5   3   1

First Graywolf Printing, 2013

Library of Congress Control Number: 2013931481

Cover design: Jeenee Lee Design

Cover art: Zurbaran, Francisco de (1598–1664).
Agnus Dei (Lamb of God), 1635.
Oil on canvas, 38 x 62 cm.
Museo del Prado, Madrid, Spain.
Photo credit: Scala/Art Resource, NY.

For Jason

and

for Roan Isabel and Fiona

I no longer tend my herd
Nor have I any other work
Now that my every act is love

—Juan de la Cruz

CONTENTS

II

tell me

what you see

THE EXCHANGE

AFTERLIFE

I could only close my eyes on the blue
Shirtsleeve of leaving and understand
I was to make my own sentence. No voice

Heard as once imagined nor did she
Beckon and somehow know what I did not
Know, behind her what I loved

All the while. I stayed as long
As I could; each morning I made the mind
Work again, each evening faced the window:

This much I remember. But to solve
Where you are you must finish. Ahead a color
Best called white in a room that appears

Unlike any other. Everything used
To get there will fall away. And to look back
Is to watch the child lie down on the floor

In the exact outline and angle I once was
To see what I saw. To take on the precise edge of
How it ends is also where it begins.

I

ALREADY BROKEN

You must write as if all along a flaw
Was on the bone, one place not quite right.
Begin the story as if you knew the horse

As weak, delicate, ruin about to happen.
Walk the road backward,
Thick with trees, out through to pasture

Where the bucket hangs ready to fill,
The truck cold, the doctor still asleep.
Your knees without mud, the handbook high

Upon the shelf, the needle as it waits for the question
Not yet asked. Morning untrampled
As a room we'd never entered. Or entered

And were not seen. Entered and then
Forgiven. Entered, never moved again.

DIAGNOSIS

How to be there, still at the center
Of where you first heard—washing dishes,
Late afternoon, the window.

No noise but the clear travel of water
Over your hands. This is how you come
To know heaven, when it is no longer

Possible. The sudden tilt of landscape
Into the one direction, the telephone
Put down. Now, to say it, word by word

Before someone else does, so when you are brought
Back by a child at the table, the dog
At the door, it is to explain this world:

The meadow you meant to walk all year,
That part of the woods you've never been.

BIOPSY

Once he lies down, he says, he is afraid
There is no getting back up. Maybe
It will be that nothing ever

Is the same; you put the body down
On the adjustable bed in the room where
Those before you also came and climbed into

Clean sheets, one blanket, one pillow, and a noise
Turning into trees whispering overhead.
People dressed in the exact clothing of each other

Walk in and never look at us. He is still afraid
And so I lie down first, which is to say nothing
Except I am not him, concentrating on the manufactured

Tiles above us, which came from somewhere far
And were brought by truck or rail to this city
Where in time they were laid one by the other

To make a ceiling, sky below which we lie
Picking out stars, as the needle enters the vein,
And we search for any possible constellation, something

Familiar to name.

CHEMOTHERAPY

My friend is going through the fire on his knees,
His hands, crossing the entire field of it;
Once in a while he calls out, bewildered,

The other side unclear, wanting to just
Lie down and wait among the scattered stones.
Unimaginable heat—he pants, lost in the light

Of what keeps happening—think water, think water,
And he manages to make out one nurse
Up against the bright and it takes everything

To tell her what he needs, as if he had come upon
The one tree still standing, and understood
She promises nothing, who in her uniform

Was all that was ever asked for and who
Could hold him as he has never been held.

SETTLING

And so it might be a medium god
We are dealing with, his house
Worthless, any possibility of father

Lost in some past, the mother off playing cards.
He who is not as much as we would wish
Or as small as could be carried

Is mediocre enough to continue
As if by mistake in a chair in the dark
Basement where what is in the freezer

Will be survival until someone finally
Walks in, only no one does as each time
The approach is made yet another reason

Gets there first and so what we want
Begins again, always in the middle,
Either too large to hold it all up

Or so miniscule to do anything more
Than what has already been done, given us.

THE SON

A man goes up a mountain. He is moved by what he believes. He sees the climb as necessary, as no way out but through. He brings his son, who watches; son who still hasn't caught on. Son who has followed. Son who thinks one day he will inherit. Son who acts as if without brothers. Son who says yes to whatever is before him. Son who waits by the old rock, the low bush. Son who brought nothing but the rucksack he was given. Son who slightly moved beneath the knife. Son who saw the end of day as ecclesiastic, as blaze. Son who in time made all other sons listen to the story of the old man who got all the way up and who without looking back went over to the other side. Who disappeared as if searching for other sons. As if done. Son who walked in quiet and calm, having come back down, alone. Son for whom nothing was changed, was changed, and in the changing changed the world.

SOMEWHERE IN NEW JERSEY
IS THE CENTER

Three miles off the interstate is whatever
Heaven might be to those who dream
Of a better return. Location is utmost,

Is everything, and here faster than imagined
Exchanges are made. This, declared everlasting
By brick laid in a pasture gone fallow,

One plan vast enough to house the many
Servers required to keep track of each
Transaction. This, the place money built

So money can build. Payment begins
Which is how you go in until you forget
The name of the agency that brought you here,

Any point of reference lost enough
That value appears everywhere. Who
Would hear as you run each formula

Into the night, examine what is wrought
In the cables, the ceaseless flicker. What
Can be made with just one push: this work of wanting

More than the actual. To watch yourself
Move in and out of all that truth
And beauty—to be in debt is to remain awake.

HIGH FINANCE

You looked up and saw across the field
One who you thought also wanted, staring back
With an idea of increase, until both

Were trading in this for that, each sign
Ready to be agreed upon as if
With enough we will have covered the entire

Meadow with all possible. The uncertain
Is taken into account as each of us
Prepares for more than is necessary

To be near what is almost ours
And to watch for defect; even damage can be useful.
To have it all known, your business,

Is to persuade the world. Only
When you see others see you, do you know.

WHAT YOU HAVE TO TELL

I swore I would learn from this, the sun
Where it fell, the window looking out over
More windows and a narrow piece of river;

You'd hand over every detail, coming close
Tell exactly how it is and how it will be.
And as you spoke each machine would fade, the room

Diminish until you sat straight up, until no more
Hospital, no elevator to open
And close with its small news, no place

Outside our door where much is decided
Without us. And out of the wreckage would come
One word, one you give that makes this right,

Even easy, being all we have loved: the weight
Of a stone in the pocket, one more kiss, the drive
Home. Glorious that word putting back the pieces

As they never were, remarkably solved, unmistakable,
From your tongue, over me, the room, but then I woke
Having fallen asleep, and the word was gone.

AGAIN THE HOSPITAL

The older poet who'd been through this
Said it was like a ship we'd find
Ourselves on, one that never leaves

While in each berth a family keeps
To themselves, leans over a bed or sits
In a pulled-up chair not to miss a thing.

By each room a gown, mask, gloves to put
Our hands into, suddenly clean enough
To touch the necessary, each removal

As if it could be the last
And we descend to the cafeteria
Or lounge where others have arrived

Too tired to speak, for a small while
Away from the wrecked body casting about in sleep,
Because when we return we must again

Take up precaution against the magnitude
Of ocean just outside the window,
Where each glove worn and replaced

Gathers, like myriad birds to float and rest,
With every intention of turning back,
To be of use, but do not know how.

WHEN IT COMES

I want to be whom you close
Your eyes on, remembered into whatever
Last you think. And the stone, left,

Still there upon return. You asked me to stay
Awake and so I sit until one by one the birds
Come back, the child gone to the bus. With time

She will simply be us; the hardest part
How it does not matter. She too will carry
A box to the fresh place, sudden and uncovered

To reveal only more dirt while she watches
The ground take into its arms what she thought
She knew. Whoever remains gets to tell the story

Until it is true. Do not close your eyes, spare me
Not one thing.

GATE

which cannot open
   with you on the other side,

that would not be
   your version, instead to say

it is the workman's fault,
   the last one gone, he who did not check

his own labor, by then already paid,
   and though you heard the truck leaving

you did not call him back—
   the day slowly ticked itself out

as you looked up at any sound
   by your window on the street

stunned by each transaction
   not yours, the piano in the building beyond

again and again
   trying to make it clear,

easier to just lie down
   not to sleep, but stay with the sky

of nothing happening
   and what you wanted to say, the voice

in the machine
   which will not be erased

unless by mistake—
    it wants to be kept, heard each day

through each message
    to find the new one, to go over

and over back into entering
    where you may not have begun but are in.

SHEETROCK

As if almost too late we ripped into each other
With whatever we had: mouth, feet, fingers,
Teeth. The resolute tools of two

Lowly carpenters who wandered
In and decided to change what they saw
As longing. The contract was full

Of how we were not to look up as we tore down
To the impossible. To begin again
Is to have no idea where this will go

As we climb around each other
Raising dust. Whole sections in our hands.
To dismantle is not about surrender; the way

In is the way out. As long as
We are here, to do something. Everything.

REAL ESTATE

What we bought we bought without knowing
The underlying. A system from before, practiced
By the many, was enough. Finally the future

Put to paper and signature. After which comes
The rest of not yet. In emptiness anything
Can be born. Using just one piece

Of furniture all else is made
To appear. Sink your hands into the over
And over, hang a hat, pull up a chair,

Sit down. The bargain is to admit
Entering a space more capable
Than you. Somewhere down deep the sole rock

Still bears us and each form filled out
Is how it changes into what we own.

PRIVATE EQUITY

To put one and one together making
Two and so on. A house appears, room
With a bed in it. To configure anyway,

Even without enough information.
We work into it, the chosen. To measure
Everything out until the one who takes over

Becomes taken. This as strategy, the art
Of how we build until management
In turn builds us, elegant the logic

Used. To draw out more than what is put in.
Everyone wants beyond; even with the one
Last page as exit plan it is by return

How we will be known. To end up where we start
Again and to look as if we gained.

TO MARKET

Everyday we eat as if not coming
Back. And each time I understand,
It turns into something else. To claim

The information was always there
Is masterful. The aisle is walked
And for each decision made, another

Unmakes. Haunts, as even with one look
It will come home with you. Everything open, nothing
Closed, all lights on. How capable we tell

Each other. From the start we were
Headed toward loss; we eat as if we might
Run out. When asked what it would mean to be

Done with not enough she could only see the end
Of beautiful. Of what it meant to cover.

LOVE POEM

Which cannot be written tries anyway—
From one room to another, each time startled
And does not want to hear of the already

Passed through, the country of before.
Poem that at each door believes itself
In the room closest to the end

Where finally everything will be gone over,
Dismantled, held up, carefully laid back down
While talked into the beauty which can turn

In a minute. To hear of every other
Poem written is to begin
Revision and what cannot be left enough

Alone and so the lovers look at each other
Until none else can come near. Poem
Which never wanted anything but this

Tries anyway, so brave, unable to know where
She heads; unwrapping until only a gift
Which cannot be given as it cannot be let go.

WHERE WE ARE BEING
WHAT WE MADE

the night undid the bed
while we followed the snake
perfect your feet at my head
my feet in your mouth as if
in some forest a clearing
held back not by fire but
by abandon
and how the end is all about
what we do not yet know
save how we are what we make
which means there is no place
to break what happens
into seeing it is enough

SUMMIT

As you rise you must remove any sign
Of rising: footprint, a branch displaced,
The shifted rock. To arrive is to leave

The way behind you unchanged, as the cold dawn
Picks over what is left. Up in regions
Not yet named, where scattered quartz

Betrays a vein private with gold, where antlers
Locked and died in struggles of domain,
The last ones still against the sky

Show the way out. In such air
Is no room for mercy. Days when we go up
The mountain, then down, only to head up

Again. Up to the edge, hurrying
To get however much done before weather.

SEEKING ALPHA

Praise for the one who can take us above
The merely saved. Without risk everything
Is fixed; the added, or taken away, must be

Explained and to stare at the screen
Of available numbers is already to depend
On how you hunt for more. When what you know

Does not match what you want it is fair
To find an enemy; to get by
No longer an option. Each move makes evident

What is not yet done. The exponential
Sets in. The torrent is the torrent
With you or without you. All that happens

Turns into the reason. And to leave behind
Who got you inside is only the beginning.

CLOSER

(Abraham, after)

It was to figure out how far you would have
Let me. Not as the actual reason, but study
Of the gap between us. A trade on what

Might appear. The bet was how near I could get
Without changing. At the utmost no one else
And none watching. Except what develops

In the midst of how you might not be
What I want which means you could be
Even more. Pure profit. Eventually

You might be made. I keep taking you
Off the table and starting over. I once loved
What I brought to the market;

Now I just want to go home
With something I did not come here with.

II

BIRD AT A WINDOW

Beyond is a brightness
I am not equal to

Yet what I see
Turns into what I want—

To bring nothing but this body
To pass through

The one thing between
Myself and what I crave,

Almost done, the world a ruin
Of leaves, winter at the throat,

My song over and over until
So familiar I can do

What I am about to do
While you who rise from the table

And walk from room to room
Will remember only the sound

Of what cast herself through
All that glass, instead of the song

That was sung until finally
You would ask to know more.

ATHEISM

in my mouth you are what I wanted to say
bedclothes taken up in small handfuls
clutched and spent like waves of an ocean

where I have gone beyond the original
plan to travel the shape back to the point
you began it was to follow the whole length

and take in by tongue every first thing
up to that edge where I might have kept you
just before you came to be nowhere

the only noise being me until done
going past the shore where this will never
happen again you in my mouth with nothing

but my own arm to save me from the fall
back as I lean into the work I have made
of such a journey of moving toward

ANALYSIS

Every time I begin with the story of a man
Willing to kill his son. Tell me what I need
To know. Simple as possible

Is wanted and should not take the many words
Already used. Each of us as animal believes
Itself last until out of some oblivion

Comes forth a child, what we were made for,
Enough to continue the whole way to you.
This, where risk is born: how much

To forget in order to live. Every time I go
I go through the steps, the climb of man and boy until
Down they come, neither with proof. But how the mountain

Is revealed as each now descends a different face,
One toward any new land, the other home to bed.

EAT WHAT YOU KILL

Responsibility is making certain
Nothing is leftover. In the utmost clearing
Where you find yourself after all

That ability, is not much light
To work by. Also, whoever watches
Is in the condition of waiting. Employment

Of what you know goes into this, metal
Tailored for your palm alone, each tool
Managed so your good luck gets spread around

Enough to explain any result, to consider
Any tremble. This last animal does not want you
Or to be you, only to know

What you want. To use the entire body
Is to kneel down; her bones are the price
Of information. What reveals wilderness

Undoes wilderness; in your hands
The instruments for which you will be known
Work even without you. Each morning

The leather bag prepared so you can talk yourself
Backward into whatever derives
From settling in with the grass; so many are the eyes on the one

Hint of prey, intent on how to eat beyond
The temptation of leaving just enough
Again for desire, even worship.

ENOUGH

Men I know go and do not come back
As if they want us on shore, thinking
Of them. I have seen how far they look

For what might not belong, darkness
Against the wave. To distinguish the one
Site of wrong is to enter into some triumph

Of taking apart. Do not loosen
What you know into the water; every tide
Delivers the unfastened. What was done

With the provided was to be for everyone;
The pieces put back together only show
How we who wait for a sign should use

The already here. How have we not understood:
There is no answer; there was no question.

THE SUIT

She said take it off slowly so I can
Master when it begins; I want to watch
How you work button by button through

Each skillful undertaking and so he moved
As if to include her but she would not touch
Or help with jacket or tie, determined

To solve from where he comes and also
To learn the color of how he can disappear
Into the sea of more and more

Black. She is tired of thinking
Further. This time everything off until the firmament
Shows up. Upon which she puts down the compass

Of her body to lie along the pressed
Cloth and slip into all that dark material
Each arm, wrist against each cuff to see how

It is done.

GIVEN PORNOGRAPHY

All this work leads to holding both
At once. In the midst of the crowd
A woman services two men, serves

Might be a kinder word but we want this
Explicit. Pressing a way through
To some bed or stage or platform is what

We do. And as she rises her body against
Each of them this makes the argument
Of resolution, of unlike moving into like

Until finally everything is the same.
We keep in time; this is not elsewhere.
Nowhere is the center more not the point,

What hand belongs to whom and where.
And to take turns and to bear
That someone goes first, which can never be

Exact or equal, is how faith must come
Into all that touch. Do not be astonished;
She has placed herself to be lost,

To be eaten while eating, a darkening
Bruise of too much, a guide of
Figuring which door to push against,

Already open. We watch for the ending
Not wanting it to end. What to know
That we did not before, save the ungodly

Angles. To do while being done. Polite the mirror
With anything possible; it is not about
Who wants whom more but you cannot help wondering

What happens to her, she who has been caught
As if between slides of glass—her body so useful.
What comes of each entrance given

Like bread to taste, to begin each day
As if starting over, considering what she has made
Of herself for herself by herself; and how

You could never have been her, until now, quiet
As a church, holy as a trinity, until just
Now the noise of trying to get it right.

ONLINE AGAIN

I know what you search, going further
Than promised, your refusal to look up
As if something might never be found;

Leaning into familiar buttons, whole days
Lost to the spare room just off the hall
Certain none will hear the chair, the deep tilt

And rapture of a self amid so much.
The ready hands as if in prayer, your hair falling
Forward at each next site you cannot believe

Your luck: she says she wants you with everything
You have as you enter her flat kingdom of bed
And lamp enough you think yourself saved

For the wife who later comes to you, steadfast
Each time, only does not know where to begin.

TURNING AWAY

I stand in front of my father's work;
How I look for myself and bring my story
And still it is not heard. Nothing here

To tell me what to believe. Nothing
But color, shapes he has seen,
Taken for meaning. Frames, a roomful

Of what was done without me. Once a man
And woman lay under the many stars
In a moment of one particular

Over another, which becomes the way
Of the world, which is why he left
Again and again, which is how she kept me

Until it was time. With all I have
I approach each painting. If I stare long enough
Something begins to move. If I look away, even then

The image refuses to leave; wherever I turn,
Always in the middle of all that white.

PRESERVATION OF CAPITAL

Risk as part of the equation means
You go nowhere without it. In one pocket
The noise of plenty; the other, dread. Each coin

Brought forth is explained
As necessary. You find yourself at the bank
Of a river where everyone gathers; you put

Children at your feet, divide the bread
While evening points out the already done.
And even when the basket holds nothing

The child considers everything and still
Duplicates until you believe
In your own redemption. No matter what you keep: from her,

For her, all that might go wrong, all you work
Into what actually is remembered last.

THAT WHICH GATHERS US IN

We thought it longing that brought us
To the fire. Out from the trees, the wait over
Because of possible light. The stumble

Into a clearing and toward what flickers,
Watching the shapes cast as we both come near.
The burning may already know how much it takes,

But I could only draw so close
Until I had to look up at stars; what is strewn above
Being easier than where we keep staring

Into flames, each in their own version
Of what we bring to these rocks. The blaze
So great the eye must turn away in order

To see again. And when I look back into your face
It is nothing but delay; dark closing in fast.

SPREAD

when you did not come did not
make arrangements when no sound was

nothing else but to do it
myself

when you did not when there was no cover
save me

already there for you
in the reach of night

scattered on the bed
with no otherwise but

this array the plot of which
so wants to be known

if only to explain distance
between one and another

as outcome
as wrong prediction again

until in the dark I turn I adjust
even without you

to still be the point
of your approach

much like under a sky to know
if one can take in all the stars

WHAT YOU WAIT FOR

She is everything imagined, down
To each wristbone, the curve of her back.
It cannot be this simple;

To close the book, to stand and pull on the coat
Your brother brought to the hospital,
To peer into the mirror a last time

Before you turn to shut the door
And step into the extraordinary air.
All this life in order to find

One who finally will not leave
Your side, and how she leans toward where she can whisper
Into your ear exactly what you wanted

When first you saw her
At the back of the room, looking up
From her table, her black dress suspect

In shadow, each goddamn time
You thought the light only a trick,
While the unbelievable red of her mouth

Was to understand the land of her skin,
The stop of her skirt precisely into everywhere,
Hair as it falls onto your shoulder,

Down your back a rain you cannot taste,
Her eye on something that moves
Outside the window, something that makes itself

Like a dove as she sets down the drink
To search for the one place
To put herself into your outspread arms.

FINALLY HE SPEAKS ABOUT DYING

For a long time we have been in this car,
His hands on the wheel, the sun
Finishing behind the building

And a couple walks by, tucked into one coat
As if against a wind; I am not sure
If he has seen them, but it goes on

This talk of his and I do not watch
His body anymore, the light being
What it is, already going. He repeats

He wants to do this alone
But will do everything they tell him
And will do nothing more than that

While now and then traffic comes
From up behind then veers around
As we sit into dark, streetlight not yet

Started, his head against the window
Like a bird, waiting; we have been at this
For hours as the light changes, trying to love

What has not yet been written and then
We are still here when the couple turns back;
They were only walking around the block

Or maybe they return because the snow
Has begun and from this sudden world
The unbroken comes, and nothing is wasted.

WHEN I CALL YOU

that was me who wandered out to the light
in the hall left on as way of promise
the house so large no one remembered

I spoke to the light as if called
pronounced your name only once as was
learned and then again backward as if

to address how much I could not bring
myself to see the nothing I am in for
as when the question is not asked

there is no answer so if I call you
do not come as though all along you knew
instead please arrive to prove at least

once how you got to be
not even here in order for us to want you

LUCY MADE A MASK IN REHAB

In some great fury the hollows shaped
Where eyes would have been, then the mouth
So one could see everything

By what was missing. She worked in the hurry
Of how a bell would soon ring, the session
End. To make the form as if it was

To be the last, left behind, hung up on the wall,
Done. To look through to the other side, to abide
What happens, and also does not happen;

Somewhere to live while waiting. This time
She did not come back. The longed-for
Never finds us, never beauty; instead how to move

Toward revelation and keep unstartled
Enough to remain. How to want to want to stay.

DARK HARBOR

(after Mark Strand)

In your night without end, in your soaking dark
You wear the suit that cannot help
Even when you lie down; too much trouble

To take things off only to put them on again
Ready to walk once more down the street
Where not one person moves, not one light

To cross under. A motel kneels at the end
Of the parking lot; the ocean beats its head
Against rock, rock that remains no matter

How many times rope or engine are laid to it,
Young men after midnight looking
To break open what they can. And so you pass by

Those who are in time forgiven for all
They once again could not hold back.

MOVING IN THE ALMOST

From some distance I have come
By the only way, past the church upon the hill,
The village clock and shuttered windows,

Down the street that leads to where you live,
To each house until it is the simple
Outline of where you might be;

From the road to the gate to the door,
From the door to the room to the bed.
In the bed a figure turning. The moon

Poured out. One finger to reach
The farthest edge until you wake and I look
Hard into your face as if never seen before

And it is enough to make you rise,
Leave behind the room, the door,
The gate click as you walk out

And follow me to where I go. Now it is you
Who enters until you are leaving. Back and forth
We move as if at each point we will be done.

THE ONE TURN THAT MAKES
THE NEW WORLD

Maybe the light from a small window
Tucked at the utmost eave of the barn
Could be misunderstood; if only I had pulled

In by the other way or not looked up
Against such darkness. The animal I brought
Into this no longer mine: the task

Each day was to confine enough, from harm
Or from each other as night loosens
Over the assemblage. But in the pasture

One wrong step was taken. And those who remain
Are weary, heads low, torment nowhere
To be seen, not even in the illumination

Of men who have come to help,
Who behind the double doors keep watch
By the body so it does not become

Anything for those who scavenge. To follow back
The acts of blood right up to the locked stall
And light where each shaft lands precisely again

Through the again. The horse was in the snow,
The rock was underfoot; all the unknowables
Made whole and apparent by one who stumbled.

DOMINION OVER THE
LARGER ANIMAL

How many times I have provided
For your death; the apple turned one way
Then the other, an arrangement made,

The softer ground. To hold your head
As if this mattered, to say what I think
Essential into your ear,

To watch the eye look everywhere to find
What it does not know it looks for.
To fasten you down in the one place

Where no one can say anything more,
Being nothing else but breath leaving,
While the man with the needle stands by

Until the signal of how it is time. To believe
I know what will happen next, to leave the hill
As the body stiffens, to pass each blossom

Of blood in the snow as if I understood
All I was capable of.

LOOKING FOR BATAILLE

The book comes down off the highest shelf,
The unbearable cover swiftly opened
Onto more suffering, which says begin

This time from the onset, the garden thought left
Intact yet where a particular wind continues
Its work among the trees. After what is taken out

On each other we cannot help but look
Even as we wonder where to go next; what
Are you afraid of—how I enter the wound

Each time to remember I am not you,
Back and forth to watch exactly what it is
That happens. And what I bring can kill,

For in your eyes is she who still wants
To go so far we will forget enough to do it again.

STATUE OF VICTORY
HALFWAY UP THE STAIR

(after Rilke)

Whatever is missing draws us in. To move
Toward the absent with an idea
Of otherwise; if only we had been there

Before all that damage. How we cannot
Help looking, an argument of too much
Beauty, imagining the hands; did it begin

In the face, the unknown head. And then the body
After, the breaking down. We walk around
In order to see what is no longer there

Prepared to answer anything
But instead the child who is with us believes
It was meant to end just so: without arm, foot or brow

And already wants to know where we go next.
Each particular as intended. What could have been.

AS DISCIPLE

I was first to believe and gave
My mouth, anything I could find
To be in front of whoever wandered in

And wanted to watch. Still, whatever
The exchange from tongue to tongue becomes
My doubt, realm which cannot be worked out,

Which keeps turning in order to see
Itself and more territory where much uprising
Is used as part of the story

Told one to the other. And into the night
Of your hair I bring what cannot be
Helped even if it accumulates

Into how much I wanted you
To fill my hands with all you know of me.

FROM STONE

Perhaps she called out for him to undo
What was around her. Or he found himself
Cutting the relentless into smaller, into

Meaning, into weight. What begins the fall;
Who first saw the path made clear, each tool
Practiced in the dark or the last space left

Which could open enough. Did she climb
Out over his dusty and fearful hand,
Or did he pull her from the still place,

The ache until one caught against the other.
Piece by piece was recognized. Beauty
As the way through. But what is done to the stone

Is also the stone. How much does he take
Before we can no longer bear to look.

ACCIDENT

Up on the mountain as she rose above
Treeline came the unexpected bodies:
The woman slightly burned, the man curled

Against her in one last concern
Of knowing. What to do with this sight
Said she to the no one there,

How you must not go too far up into
Good weather. Perhaps they had no idea
How to pay attention. How much did they want;

At what point were they going to turn back
Down. To be close enough to see beyond
Her own desire is how she must now live.

LEVERAGE

For us to be positioned well requires
Margin; I made a small room, a belief
In more. A simple debt where plenty can

Build until no longer in the place
We started; our domain without end as end
Outdoes any other outcome and we are not easy

With our own sum. I do not want to talk
About the weight of the actual;
Someone said to talk is to kill the thing

We make. What to do with the known
Passed from each to each. What keeps us then
Is all that might be lost; after my hand, before yours,

Lying between us now measured, counted,
Each time a little less to live with.

GETTING TO THE END

I went out for what you needed
Even when you did not ask. Went like
A dog, and maybe it wasn't significant

Or maybe it was just for the noise
But what else to do with so much time
Already spent. One body leans against another

Waiting for the other to move.
Landscape so precise, the still life
Of how we keep. And us in it, until

We said above all we loved
How that happened. What did we sign enough to bear
Agreement, to bear forgetting, until

One of us is suddenly through and the audacity
Of how it could be either way.

MAN OVERBOARD

This was not the plan. The once-ready rope
Now moved like a sudden snake, the boat
A wild animal. Never had he seen

How she might be without him. Never had he thought
Himself in the water as she shook
Through the tumbling ocean, her steering

Gone. Now he could not remember what it was
He wanted. Only to turn all this into
Simply heading for home, the fendered wharf

Mostly lit, the harbormaster nodding.
He was ready to be done with each pivot
Of hull, shroud, and sail. Still the waves hover

One by one, move on—now to stay long enough
To watch everything ever learned pull away
On a boat that could not turn to save him.

IT NEVER GOES AWAY

I will try to know your death exactly
As you do. The moon has shown up tonight,
Coin in the palm of one we wait for, sunset

Long gone. So hard this practice to wake
Into no more light, not even in the place
You left it. Then each morning comes

And you are followed by the rise
Of landscape everywhere. We never know
How much it takes, this business

Of departure; you stare into ocean
Outdone by all you want. Enough
Of what continues. Here it comes again,

The turning of dark and dirt, unable to stop;
Love, even with everything to be sad about.

YOU SAID IT WAS NOT

About the dying but carrying us through
What we become at the shore while you turn
Toward the waves. One after another

We come, each wandering the coastline
To get here, some arriving late with much to say
While others go off to be alone,

And in this last light we gather
As if by some fire we build without you
But with possibility in mind,

And we move just enough to stay
Awake which is what we believe you wanted
When you said you were so afraid

We would forget. Instead it is you who no longer
Remember as you turn away and into
The wind the water the open boat

And how you get to be everything,
Get to be what is gone and wanted back.

BIRD LEFT BEHIND

As for her, the circumstances must be ordinary
And so the return. Door unlocked. The path mowed
Right to the oiled gate, the pasture

Cleared of stone and alder. All untouched
Enough to enter. The man or woman
Off down the valley or working above

Treeline. No other sound but a few strays
Hurrying through the dusk as if the end
Will begin, certain and with nothing

More to say. She does not know she does not know.
Having come back to find her kind
And none being left she took herself up

Into a tree unclear what to do next save only
Sing the song she wanted sung back to her.

PALMS FACING OUT AND AWAY
FROM THE BODY

After my mother said do not come back
Until he gives you good money I went
To the place of men in jackets waiting

For the bell, the trade, what might make
Enough to sell. How did they come to be first,
Able to leave before break of day the sleeping

Who depend as if somewhere is written
Redemption can be had. Managing excess
Is what the market does and in the open

Outcry and face to face will be a few
Who walk away with much. I look for one
Who will buy what I owe among the many

Who take from each other what I cannot
Understand until everything being profit
Or loss is a promise of someone on the other

Side. And then to be nimble for he
Who drives out risk does not look back;
I will let him borrow when his hand

Is where I can see it. The bull does not
Die easily, runs up and down the fence
And wants you near when there is talk

About distress and what could be done
When found. Closing in on that which is the same
And that which has strayed, the bid

And the ask. And I who wonder
Does she wait for me to round the bend
Come home with a brochure instead—

I search for the one who leaves with less,
I shadow him with something to change
Quick before the close of day, before the pit

Grows quiet, empty, each terminal dark
With how today is not tomorrow,
The floor strewn with paper:

Husks broken into radiance,
No longer static inside the sleeve, gold
Let loose, grain for the cow, field, and city—

And into the lavish night goes the chosen,
Hungry to seek what is capable
And for the unleashing it cannot wait.

I HAVE TALKED TOO MUCH

About the end and now it is a room
In which only white waits, as if for an error
To appear. I have gone over the book

Of pictures which moves like a corridor
Made more narrow as each door closes
In the hall which asks you

To finally open the last onto what
Was longed for and there he sits staring
At the math, the equation,

The blackboard which could have held anything
And should have said everything
But maybe all along the point was not to

Look, not even approach. We are not able
To handle what we are capable of. At the end,
Only information, no longer in need of a host.

OUR HOUSE

As the leaves turn their backs on us
And the lilac gives over to dusk, nothing
Is ever certain, not even the house, stubborn

In twilight as it outlasts the grove
It was wrestled from. Those left behind,
The oak and ancient elm, lean against each other

As if in consent. Out of dirt, out of
Some small mistake, comes the seedling;
It too has learned to watch, as we walk in and out

Of what wilderness was, and will again become,
As we enter our home, the way we enter love
Returning from elsewhere to call out
Each other's names, pulling the door closed behind us.

PAY ATTENTION

I can only do what is here. But you
Have an entire congregation of choice,
If you are who they say. The child
Believes you cannot be, just

Doing nothing. I watched, I asked
But also without going very far.
I took care of myself. I took care
Of myself, thinking much too often

I took care of someone else.
Everything feels like payment. In fact
We come into this paying. And you, who are
Nowhere to be found, who make

No noise, who cannot be smelled or tasted,
Wander through with all of us wanting you
At the same time. Oh to be wanted
Like that, for you to pull up a chair

And let your knees touch mine.
For one moment not to answer
The other call, not to look
Past my shoulder when something else moves.

UNBOUND

(Isaac, after)

This being beyond the expected, this
Still here. First the almost, then the animal
Which was to save or at least provide

Another chance, but now will not allow
Any near, even as unfettered. My father, finished
With sacrifice, left. Many have come to this field

To wait. The more they wait the more
They also leave, only to return again with others
Until the field is filled with waiting. And here am I

Who withheld nothing. And there the white
Always in the tree. You go
Where you need to go until it does not

Matter. You do not matter. There is
The window. Open. Now go through.

NOTES

This book's epigraph is in response to Louise Glück's "Vita Nova."

"The Son" was compelled by the regimes of Presidents George H. W. Bush and George W. Bush.

"Somewhere in New Jersey Is the Center" is another take on the New York Stock Exchange's Data Center in Mahwah, New Jersey. The line "Payment begins / Which is how you go in" is based on a line from Leonard Bernstein's opera *A Quiet Place*.

"What You Have to Tell" was in part inspired by Vladimir Nabokov's story "The Word."

"Again the Hospital" is in gratitude to Donald Hall's poem "The Ship Pounding."

The end of the poem "To Market" uses for its last question text from Mark C. Taylor's book *Mystic Bones*.

For another definition of "Seeking Alpha" please see *Barron's Dictionary of Finance and Investment Terms*.

"Lucy Made a Mask in Rehab" is for Lucy Grealy.

The poem "Accident" was in part inspired by stories told by Tom Perry and Beth Loffreda.

"It Never Goes Away" is part of a call and response to Jason Shinder's poem "At Sunset."

ACKNOWLEDGMENTS

Grateful acknowledgment is made to the editors of the following publications in which some of these poems first appeared: *AGNI,* the *American Poetry Review, Boston Review, Columbia Magazine, Denver Quarterly, Granta, Harvard Review,* the *Nation,* the *New Republic,* the *New Yorker, Open City,* the *Paris Review, Poetry, Provincetown Arts, Salamander, Slate, Tin House,* and *Tuesday: An Art Project.*

"Turning Away" appeared in *Fatherhood,* ed: Carmela Ciuraru, Everyman's Library, 2007.

"Our House" appeared in the *Poetry Speaks Calendar,* 2008.

With much appreciation to Mark C. Taylor, Robert Pollack, and National Public Radio.

And also to Carmela Ciuraru, Timothy Donnelly, and Jeffrey Shotts for their support, and to the many givers of care throughout the writing of this book.

Also many thanks to Dahlia House and to Sarah Dudley Plimpton.

Finally, the deepest gratitude to my family.

SOPHIE CABOT BLACK is the author of two previous poetry collections, *The Descent,* winner of the Connecticut Book Award, and *The Misunderstanding of Nature,* winner of the Norma Farber First Book Award. She lives in New England.

This book is based on a design by Tree Swenson.
It is set in Baskerville type with Goudy titling by BookMobile
Design & Digital Publisher Services, Minneapolis, Minnesota.
Manufactured by Versa Press on acid-free
30 percent postconsumer wastepaper.